602
T24m

AGE5480-1

CL
7100

Traditional Crafts from
NATIVE NORTH AMERICA

Traditional Crafts from
NATIVE NORTH AMERICA

by Florence Temko

with illustrations by Randall Gooch
and photographs by Robert L. and Diane Wolfe

 Lerner Publications Company • Minneapolis

To Dennis, Janet, Ellen, and Stephen

Over the years, I have tucked away bits of information in my files
that have contributed to my fascination with crafts. They were
gathered mainly from personal meetings, books, magazines,
libraries, and museums. I regret it is no longer possible to
disentangle these many and varied resources, but I would like
to acknowledge gratefully and humbly everyone who has helped
to make this book possible.   —Florence Temko

Text copyright © 1997 by Florence Temko
Illustrations copyright © 1997 by Lerner Publications Company

Library of Congress Cataloging-in-Publication Data

Temko, Florence.
    Traditional crafts from native North America / by Florence Temko ;
  with illustrations by Randall Gooch and photographs by Robert L. and
  Diane Wolfe.
      p.   cm.—(Culture crafts)
    Includes index.
    Summary: Provides instructions for making such traditional North
  American Indian crafts as dreamcatchers, beadwork, and cornhusk dolls.
    ISBN 0-8225-2934-3 (alk. paper)
    1. Indian craft—Juvenile literature. 2. Indians of North America—Industries—
  Juvenile literature. [1. Indian craft. 2. Handicraft] I. Title. II. Series.
  T T22.T46 1997
    745.5'089'97—dc20   96-4973

Manufactured in the United States of America
1 2 3 4 5 6 – JR – 02 01 00 99 98 97

CONTENTS

WHAT ARE CRAFTS?

All over the world, people need baskets, bowls, clothes, and tools. People now make many of these things in factories. But long ago, people made what they needed by hand. They formed clay and metal pots for cooking. They wove cloth to wear. They made baskets to carry food. We call these things "crafts" when they are made by hand.

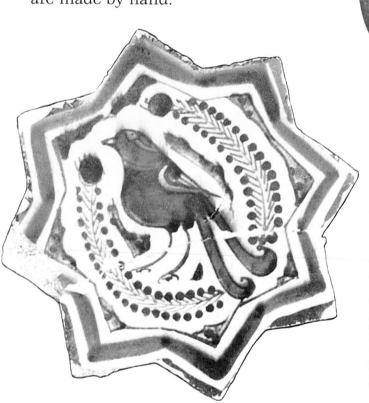

Grandparents and parents taught children how to make crafts. While they worked, the elders told stories. These stories told of their family's culture—all of the ideas and customs that a group of people believe in and practice. Children learned these stories as they learned the ways of making crafts. They painted or carved symbols from those stories on their crafts.

Year after year, methods and symbols were passed from parents to children. Still, each bowl or basket they made would look a little different. A craft made by hand—even by the same person—never turns out the exact same way twice.

People who are very good at making crafts are called artisans. Many artisans still use the old methods. They make useful things for themselves and their homes. Today, some artisans also sell their crafts to earn money.

Left to right: A painted tile from Turkey, a Pueblo Indian pitcher, a pot from Peru, and a porcelain dish from China

MATERIALS AND SUPPLIES

Some of the suggested materials for the crafts in this book are the same as those used by Native American artisans. Others will give you almost the same results. Most materials can be found at home or purchased at local stores. Check your telephone book for stores in your area that sell art materials, craft supplies, and teachers' supplies. Whenever you can, try to use recyclable materials—and remember to reuse or recycle the scraps from your projects.

MEASUREMENTS

Sizes are given in inches. If you prefer to use the metric system, you can use the conversion chart on page 58. Because fractions can be hard to work with, round all metric measurements to the nearest whole number.

FINISHES

The crafts in this book that are made from paper will last longer if you brush or sponge them with a thin coat of finish. These are some choices:

White glue (Elmer's or another brand) is the most widely available. Use it at full strength or dilute it with a few drops of water. Apply it with a brush or small sponge. (The sponge should be thrown away after you use it.) White glue dries clear.

Acrylic medium is sold in art supply stores. It handles much like white glue. You can choose a glossy (shiny) finish or a matte (dull) finish.

9

NATIVE NORTH AMERICAN CRAFTS

Indians have lived on the North American continent for thousands of years. Through time they developed into many different tribes, which can be grouped by culture areas. Tribes in each area may be related by similar ways of life. Crafts are one way that Indians connect the traditions of the past with the present and future.

MAJOR CULTURE AREAS

The Plains area lies between the Mississippi River and the Rocky Mountains, and it stretches as far south as the Gulf of Mexico. Plains Indians emphasize decoration in their crafts. They often use feathers, beads, and porcupine quills.

The Eastern Woodlands is a heavily forested area that stretches from the U.S. and Canadian Atlantic coast to the Mississippi River. Woodland tribes make baskets and other crafts from birch, black ash, and sweetgrass.

The Southwest area includes the northern part of Mexico, as well as the states of Arizona, New Mexico, and southern Utah. Tribes in this area are known for their woven rugs and silver jewelry, as well as for their pottery.

The California-Intermountain area includes part of the southern California coast and reaches inland to the Rocky Mountains. The crafts practiced by these tribes include weaving baskets from many kinds of dried grasses.

The Northwest Coast area stretches along the Pacific coast and farther inland into the United States and Canada. Many Northwest Coast tribes carve trees into masks and totem poles. The carvings are often figures of birds and animals that are native to the area, such as ravens and whales.

The Far North, which begins at the U.S.–Canada border and extends to the Arctic Circle, is a land of cold and snowy winters. Tribes in the Far North once hunted moose, caribou, bison, and musk oxen, using the hides to make clothing. They often decorated these clothes with patterns of porcupine quills. Beading clothing is still a popular craft in the Far North.

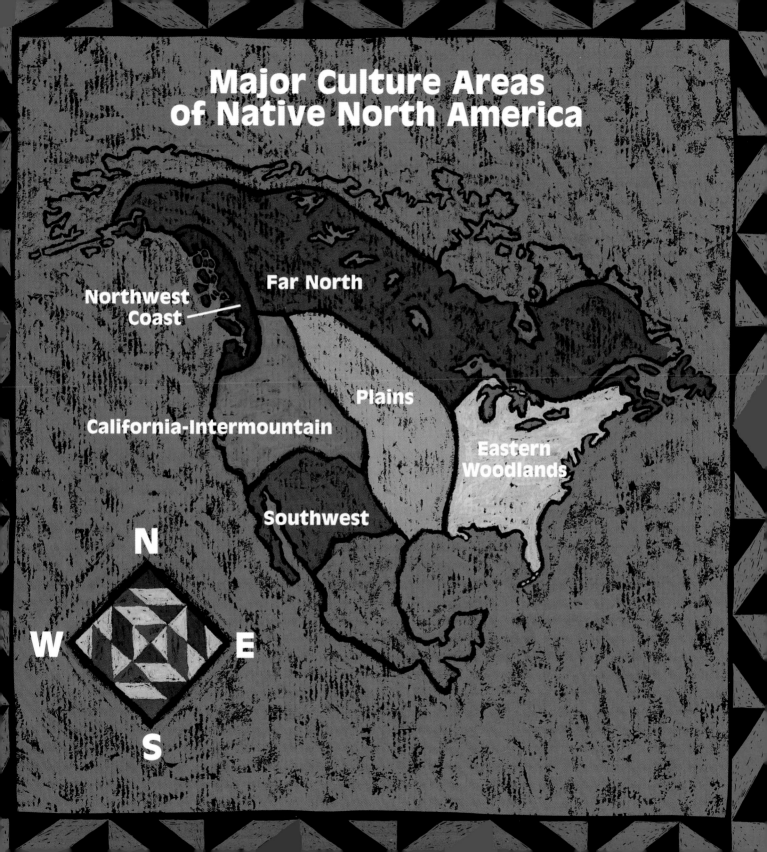

Lakota Dreamcatcher

Hang a dreamcatcher by your bed to catch your bad dreams.

LAKOTA DREAMCATCHER

The Lakota are among the Plains Indians who make circular dreamcatchers from willow tree branches, sinew, feathers, and beads. They sometimes hang dreamcatchers near where they sleep—and over the cradles of babies. They believe that good dreams go through the hole in the center,

The Lakota live in the Plains culture area. Huge herds of bison once roamed the plains, and the Lakota hunted them for meat and for leather. They sewed the hides with a tough thread made from bison sinew, the cord-like tissue that connects muscles to bones.

reaching the sleeper. But bad dreams are caught in the webbing like flies in a spiderweb.

TECHNIQUE

A dreamcatcher's knotted web—originally sinew—is strung inside a willow branch bent into a ring. The circle is decorated with feathers and beads, and sometimes with objects that have meaning for the sleeper.

This Lakota dreamcatcher was made with a traditional willow branch.

Iktome (eek-TOE-mee) means "spider" in Lakota. Iktome is also the name of a Lakota trickster. A trickster is a man who can change himself into any kind of animal or bird. He likes to trick other people, but he usually gets into trouble himself.

In one Plains Indian legend, Iktome takes the form of a spider. An old woman tricks Iktome into teaching her how to weave the dreamcatcher's web.

HOW-TO PROJECT

Dreamcatchers can be used as wall or window decorations. Look for feathers in craft stores and school supply catalogs. Feather dusters are another good source.

You need:

1 six-inch embroidery hoop
(inside ring only)
2 yards of thin string or yarn
Beads, wood or any kind
Feathers
Scissors
Pencil

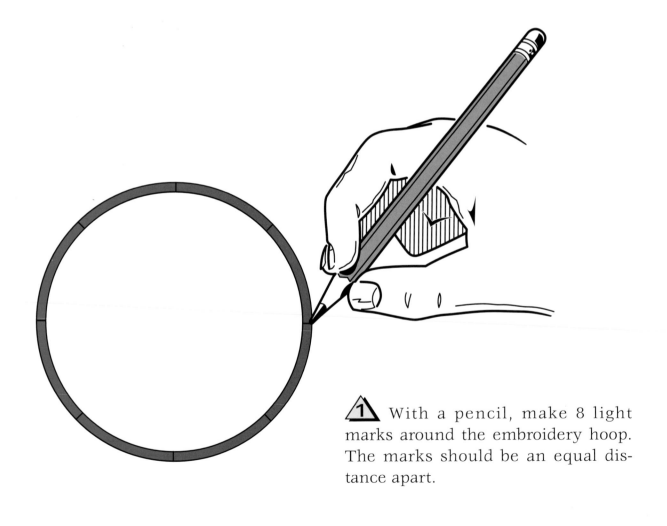

1 With a pencil, make 8 light marks around the embroidery hoop. The marks should be an equal distance apart.

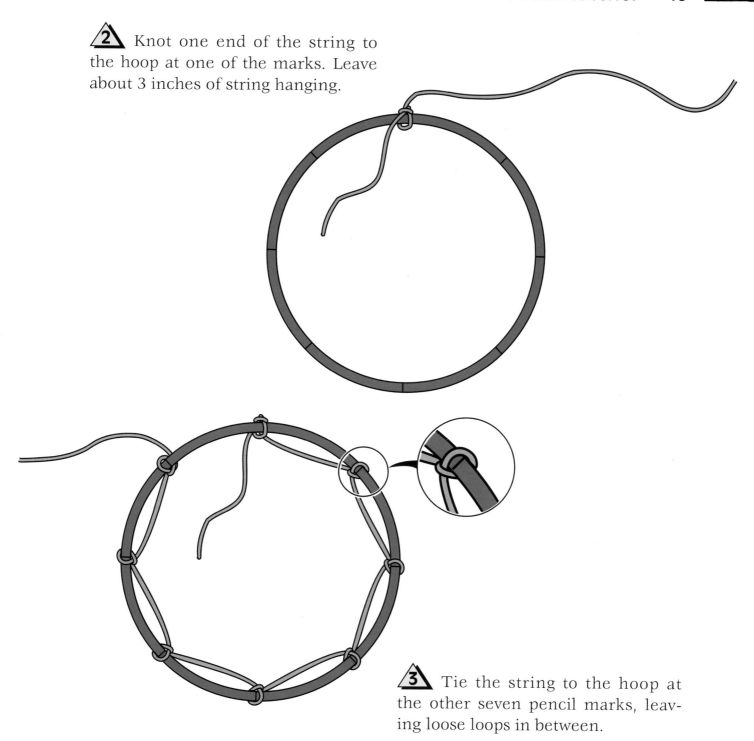

2 Knot one end of the string to the hoop at one of the marks. Leave about 3 inches of string hanging.

3 Tie the string to the hoop at the other seven pencil marks, leaving loose loops in between.

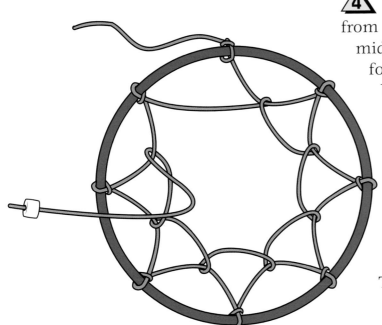

4 Continue looping the string from the middle of one loop to the middle of the next. Make three or four rows of loops, stringing a bead or two along the way.

When just a small hole is left in the center, you are ready to finish off your dreamcatcher web. Pull the string tight and knot the end of the string to the previous row. Tie another knot in the same place to prevent unraveling. Trim the string close to the knot.

5 Take the piece of string left hanging at the beginning and tie to the inside of the web, so the design is symmetrical. Again, tie a double knot and trim away any extra string.

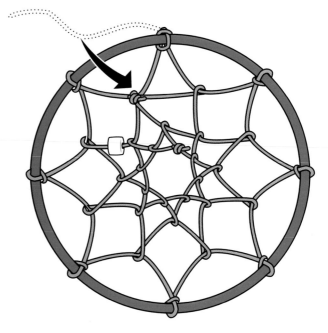

6 To make a hanger, tie a loop of string or yarn to the top of the ring. Attach feathers and beads with short strings tied to the bottom.

WHAT ELSE YOU CAN DO

Other Rings: For the embroidery hoop, substitute a 6-inch metal ring used for macramé knotting. Rings are sold in craft and needlework stores and school supply catalogs. Or make a ring from a paper plate. Pierce a hole in the middle of the plate and cut out the center, leaving only a 1-inch rim all around. Wind masking tape around the ring to strengthen it. Then weave the web with string, according to the instructions.

Blackfeet Beadwork

Once you have learned the basics of beadwork, you can decorate hats, purses, moccasins, and more.

BLACKFEET BEADWORK

The Blackfeet Nation is made up of three tribes—the Siksika, the Kainah (also known as the Blood), and the Peigan. The Blackfeet are named for the black moccasins (soft leather shoes) they made from dyed bison skins. The Blackfeet decorated the moccasins with beaded designs.

The Blackfeet have lived in the Plains culture area for hundreds of years. They made beads from elk teeth, porcupine quills, shells, and other natural materials. They obtained shells by trading with coastal tribes.

Early Blackfeet tribes made beads from natural materials. When Europeans arrived in North America, they brought glass beads in brilliant colors from Venice, Italy. They offered them to the native people as gifts or in trade. Since the early 1800s, Indians have added glass beads to the materials they use to create jewelry and embroider clothing.

TECHNIQUE

The earliest Blackfeet artisans strung beads on sinew, sewed them onto animal skins or fabric, or used a loom to weave beads into patterns. Glass beads already had holes, but in other materials holes had to be drilled with a pointed stone twirled between the palms of the hands. When thread and electric drills became available, Indian artisans were able to speed up their work.

Most Native North American tribes still decorate clothing with beadwork. Some designs are based on nature—such as the flower on this beaded bag made by a Blackfeet artisan. Other designs are based on geometric shapes and patterns.

HOW-TO PROJECT

Beaded decorations can be sewed to a headband, wristband, or purse. It's even possible to bead on a piece of strong paper, such as a grocery bag.

Beading needles are made thin, so they pass easily through beads. But you can use any kind of needle that fits through the holes of your beads.

You need:

Glass beads in red and blue, or
   2 other colors
2 saucers (to hold beads)
Graph paper
Colored pencils (red and blue,
   or other colors to match your
   beads)
Ruler
Fine-point marker
Beading needle or sewing
   needle
Nylon thread
Felt strip, 1½ inches wide by
   10 inches long
2 feet of ribbon or leather
   thong, or 1 inch of Velcro
   fastener

1 In 5 rows of squares on a piece of graph paper, shade the design you want to bead.

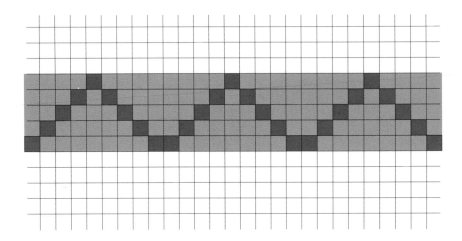

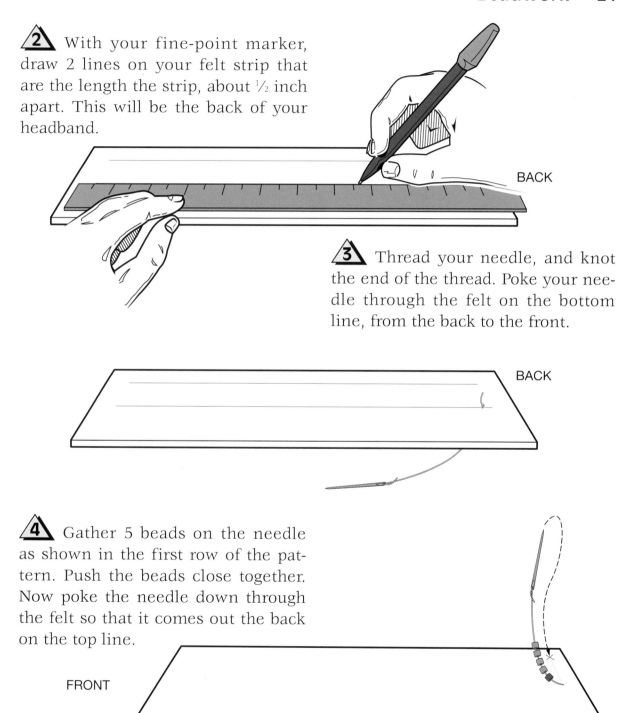

2 With your fine-point marker, draw 2 lines on your felt strip that are the length the strip, about ½ inch apart. This will be the back of your headband.

BACK

3 Thread your needle, and knot the end of the thread. Poke your needle through the felt on the bottom line, from the back to the front.

BACK

4 Gather 5 beads on the needle as shown in the first row of the pattern. Push the beads close together. Now poke the needle down through the felt so that it comes out the back on the top line.

FRONT

5 Push the needle up through the felt again, on the bottom line. The needle should come up close to your first row of beads. Then gather 5 more beads on the needle and push the needle down again, coming back through the top line.

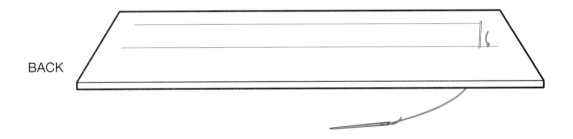

BACK

6 Continue stitching through the felt, gathering beads to match each row of your sketch. When you want to end your beadwork, take a few tiny stitches in the back of the felt or tie a knot in the thread.

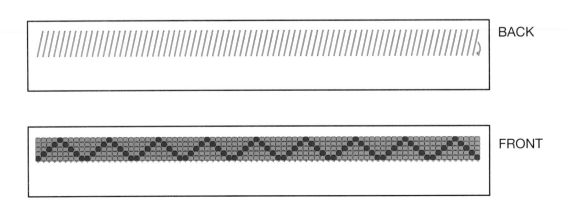

BACK

FRONT

7 To finish the headband, knot on two pieces of ribbon or leather thong, or sew on strips of Velcro.

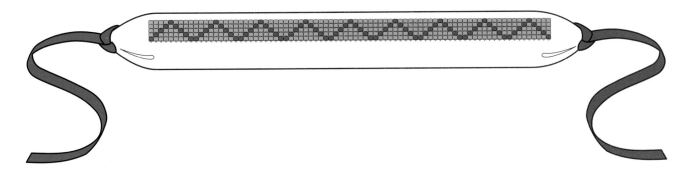

WHAT ELSE YOU CAN DO

Repeat Patterns: Repeat the pattern along the felt strip two or three more times for a longer zigzag.

Design Your Own: It's fun to design your own beading patterns. Sketch them first on graph paper, using colored pencils.

Make a Bag: Cut two pieces of felt to the same size and shape. Stitch a beadwork design to one piece. Then stitch the two felt pieces together with yarn and a large needle.

Iroquois Cornhusk Doll

The next time you eat corn on the cob, save the husks that are wrapped around the outside. They can be turned into dolls like those enjoyed by Iroquois children.

IROQUOIS CORNHUSK DOLL

Iroquois (EAR-uh-kwoy) is actually a French name for a group of six Indian nations: the Mohawk, the Oneida (oh-NYE-duh), the Onondaga (ah-nun-DAW-guh), the Cayuga (kay-YOO-guh), the Seneca (SEH-nih-kuh), and the Tuscarora (tuss-kuh-ROAR-uh). The Indian name for the Six Nations is Haudenosaunee (haw-deh-noh-SHOH-nee).

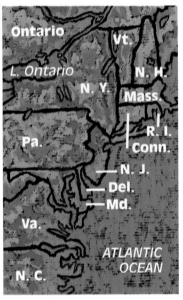

The Iroquois tribes originally lived in the northeastern part of what became the United States, in the Eastern Woodlands culture area. But they moved to reservations as far away as Oklahoma, Wisconsin, and Quebec.

To the early Iroquois, corn was the most important crop. Every year they held festivals to honor the harvest. Masks formed an important part of these festivals. The Iroquois often made masks from braided cornhusks.

TECHNIQUE

After a harvest festival, Iroquis adults sometimes tied a few cornhusks together to make dolls for their children. The Iroquois soaked the dried husks first, to make them bendable. Often husks were braided together to form the dolls arms and legs.

Iroquois Indians do not put faces on their dolls, because they believe that only the Creator can make a face.

HOW-TO PROJECT

It's best to dry fresh corn husks so that they do not split apart later. Dry the husks in the sun. They will twist and turn yellow. You may also find dried corn husks for sale in stores that sell Mexican foods.

After the husks have dried, they must be soaked to make them flexible enough for shaping. Soak the husks in warm water for about an hour. Remove from the water and pat dry.

You need:

8 corn husks, soaked for 1 hour
Towel
Thread
Scissors

1 Roll 5 to 6 soaked corn husks into a bundle. Tie the bundle with thread, about ½ inch from one end, pulling tightly.

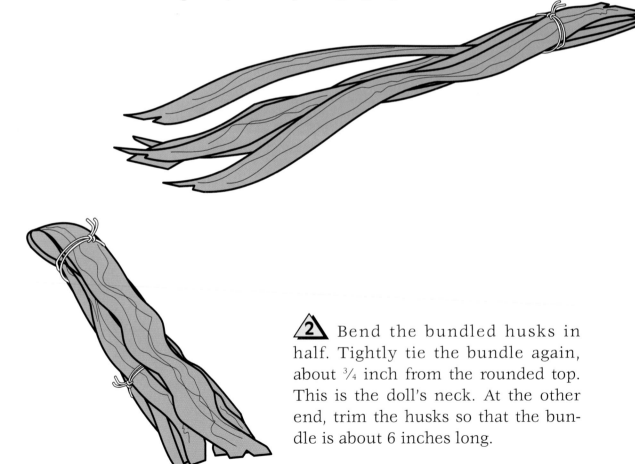

2 Bend the bundled husks in half. Tightly tie the bundle again, about ¾ inch from the rounded top. This is the doll's neck. At the other end, trim the husks so that the bundle is about 6 inches long.

3 Roll another husk tightly, so that it is about as thick as a pencil. Slide it into the bundle under the doll's neck. Tie the bundle below the rolled husk.

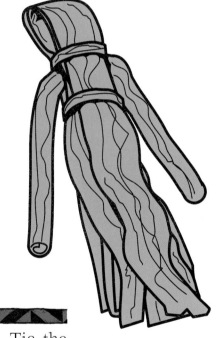

4 Hide the knotted threads with a thin strip of corn husk tied around them. If you would like the arms to be closer to the body, tie them into place with thread, which you can cut off later. Let the doll dry.

WHAT ELSE YOU CAN DO

Legs: Add legs with another rolled husk. Tie the doll at the waist and again below the rolled husk. Bend the legs down and tie the ends with thread.

Braided Arms or Legs: Instead of rolling a single husk for each piece, braid three husks together. Tie the ends.

Clothing and Hair: Clothing can be made from fabric scraps. To make hair, glue on dried corn silk or pieces of yarn.

Seminole Patchwork

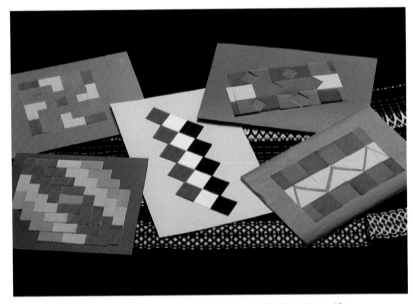

Use patchwork patterns to create original, attractive greeting cards for any occasion.

SEMINOLE PATCHWORK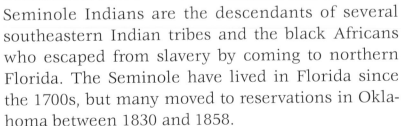

Seminole Indians are the descendants of several southeastern Indian tribes and the black Africans who escaped from slavery by coming to northern Florida. The Seminole have lived in Florida since the 1700s, but many moved to reservations in Oklahoma between 1830 and 1858.

In the late 1800s, the Seminole acquired sewing machines from traders. Seminole women began to decorate their clothing with patchwork designs.

The Seminole Indians live in the Eastern Woodlands culture area. Many live in southern Florida, where marshy lands are home to deer, bears, otters, raccoons, rabbits, turtles, and alligators.

Some patchwork designs have been passed from generation to generation, but each sewer may change the patterns slightly according to her taste.

TECHNIQUE

Seminole women sew strips of colored cotton cloth into long pieces. Then the sewers cut the pieces into sections and arrange them into designs.

Patterns are often named for the objects they resemble—such as "arrows," "lightning," or "rattlesnake." Some patterns are named after the women who create them.

Seminole women sew brightly colored strips of fabric into patchwork patterns. The patchwork decorates many items of traditional Seminole clothing, including men's shirts and women's long skirts and short capes.

HOW-TO PROJECT

Seminole sewers often use paper to design new patchwork patterns. They cut pieces of paper and shift them until they are satisfied with the arrangement. Then they copy the patterns in cloth. You can get a feel for the patchwork design technique by working with paper. Use your completed designs to illustrate a greeting card.

About gluing: To avoid bumps and bubbles, use glue very lightly. After gluing, press down on the paper or roll over it with the back of a spoon to squeeze out any air pockets.

> ### You need:
> 4 sheets colored art paper, in four different colors
> 1 sheet plain paper
> Pencil
> Ruler
> Scissors

1 From each sheet of colored paper, cut strips that are 1 inch wide and 5 inches long.

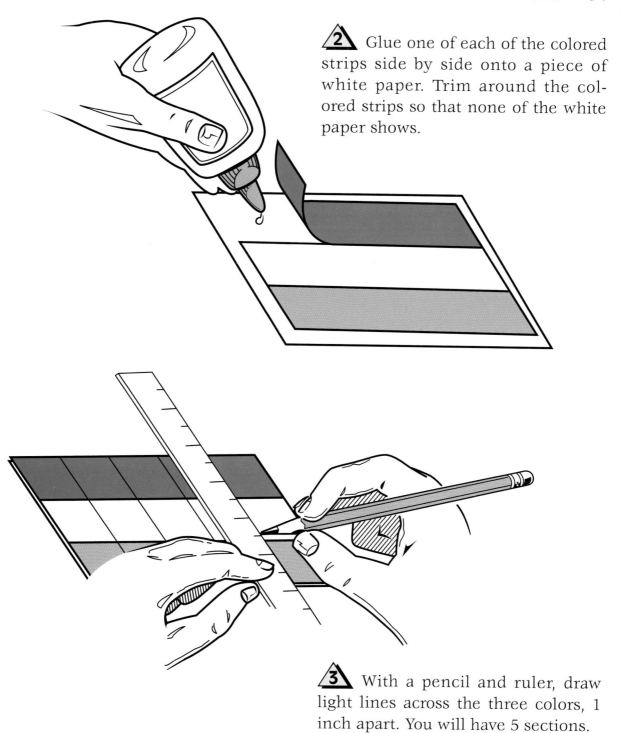

2 Glue one of each of the colored strips side by side onto a piece of white paper. Trim around the colored strips so that none of the white paper shows.

3 With a pencil and ruler, draw light lines across the three colors, 1 inch apart. You will have 5 sections.

4 Cut on the pencil lines to make 5 new three-colored strips.

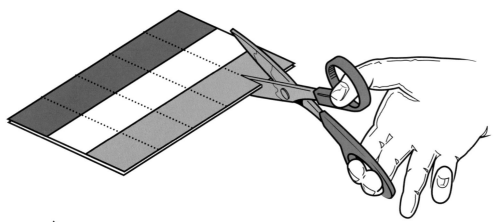

5 Fold your other piece of colored paper in half to make a greeting card. Glue the three-colored strips to the front of the card, arranging them side by side in a step pattern.

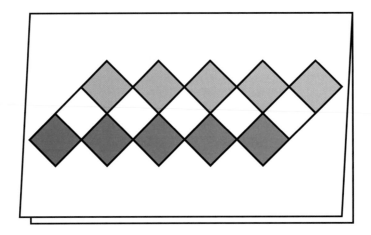

WHAT ELSE YOU CAN DO

Other Decorations: Use your patchwork designs to decorate school reports, place mats, or posters.

Cloth Designs: Once you understand the method of making patchwork designs, you may want to try using cloth. Felt pieces can be glued together with white glue just like paper. If you use cotton cloth as the Seminole do, you must sew the strips together. Cut the strips ¼-inch wider to allow for seams. You can sew bands of patchwork as decoration on clothing or place mats.

Southwestern Cascarones

Tissue paper and confetti make cascarones a festive craft.

CASCARONES

In the American Southwest, several cultures have influenced each other's craft traditions. These influences can be seen in *cascarones* (cahs-cah-ROHN-ehs)—decorated eggshells filled with

In the Southwest culture area—especially near the border of Arizona and Mexico—many cultures come together. Along with Mexicans and Mexican Americans, several Indian nations live here: the Quechuan, Yaqui, Cocopah, and Tohono O'odham. Many customs and crafts of the area show the influence of the Mexican peoples.

confetti. Cascarones made in the Tucson, Arizona, area are attached to paper cones. At celebrations called fiestas (fee-ESS-tuhs), children break cascarones on each other's shoulders, and the confetti flies out.

Cascaron is a Spanish word meaning "eggshell." Cascarones are a traditional Mexican craft that has been adapted by people living near the Arizona-Mexico border.

TECHNIQUE

Some cascarone crafters leave the eggshell plain and decorate the cones with layers of brightly colored tissue paper. Sometimes feathers, paper streamers, or ribbons hang from the cones.

Other artisans decorate just the eggshells. They paint the shells with complex designs, flowers, or the faces of a person or animal.

These cascarones have been decorated to resemble comic-book characters.

HOW-TO PROJECT

Cascarones are fun to use for party favors, or your guests can make their own. They can break them in the traditional way, or they can keep them for ornaments.

The technique of breaking eggs described below may take a little practice. Save the insides of the eggs to use for cooking.

Packaged confetti is sold in party supply stores. You can make your own by cutting colored paper into small pieces with a scissors.

You need:

Several eggs
1 sheet newspaper, 28 by 22 inches
Tissue paper, in at least 2 different colors
Confetti
Scissors
Pencil
Heavy butter knife
Bowl
White glue
Masking tape, ¾ inch wide
Various decorations of your choice:
Felt pens, glitter, metallic confetti, ribbon, colored papers

1 Hold an egg over a bowl. With a table knife in your other hand, tap the egg sharply about ½ inch from one end. Rinse the empty eggshell carefully under running water.

2 Place the eggshell on your work surface with the flat end down. Draw a face on the shell with felt pens, or decorate the shell with yarn, glitter, or other materials. Set the head aside.

3 Fold the newspaper into quarters, so that you have a rectangle measuring 11 inches by 14 inches.

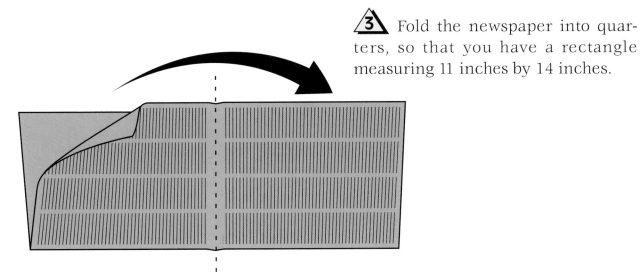

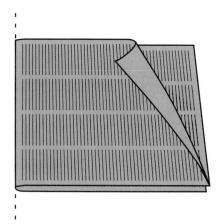

4 Draw a line 2 inches from the corner of the narrow edge at the top down to the opposite bottom corner. Crease the newspapers on that line and roll the paper into a cone. The top of the cone should be about the same size as the bottom of your decorated shell.

5 Tape the corner of the paper to keep the cone from unrolling. Cut straight across the top of the cone. Fill the cone with confetti.

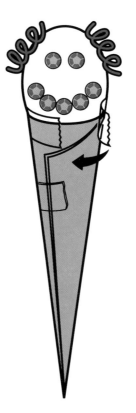

⚠️6 Attach the egg head to the cone with masking tape, covering only a narrow edge of the bottom of the egg. Decorate the newspaper cone.

WHAT ELSE YOU CAN DO

Tissue Paper Decorations: Cut long strips of tissue paper about 4 inches wide. Fold the strips in half lengthwise and make cuts along the fold, about 1½ inches long. Cover the cone with a light coating of glue. Wind the strips around the cone. Glue streamers made of tissue paper to the bottom.

Cardboard Tubes: Substitute cardboard tubes from paper towels or toilet tissue for newspaper cones.

Other Fillings: For a wedding, make bride and groom cascarones filled with rice. Give them to the wedding couple as a good luck wish. For a Halloween or birthday party, fill the paper cones with wrapped candy.

Pueblo Storyteller Doll

These storytellers' mouths are open, ready to talk or sing. Their eyes are closed because they are thinking about their stories. The children snuggle close and listen.

PUEBLO STORYTELLER DOLL

Storyteller dolls combine two Pueblo (PWEH-bloh) traditions: storytelling and pottery. Because they had no written language, the early Pueblo Indians passed on their history through storytelling. And for many hundreds of years, Pueblo Indians have made their pottery by hand. They use the brownish-orange clay found in the mountains of northern New Mexico.

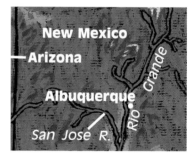

The Pueblo Indians live in 19 different pueblos in New Mexico, part of the Southwest culture area. Pueblo Indians are descended from the Anasazi (on-a-SAH-zee), whose civilization existed hundreds of years before Europeans came to North America. Like their Anasazi ancestors, many Pueblo build their homes from bricks of adobe (ah-DOE-bee)—mud or clay mixed with straw.

The Pueblo treat the clay with respect. They believe that the spirit of the clay watches over them and guides their work. Each pueblo (village) has its own designs, such as lizards, snakes, and bears.

Helen Cordero, from Cochiti pueblo in New Mexico, created the first storyteller dolls in the 1950s. Since that time, as many as 175 Pueblo Indian potters have designed brightly colored storyteller figures.

TECHNIQUE

After the Pueblo potters have collected buckets of clay, they push the clay through screens to remove twigs and rocks. Next, the clay is mixed with a fine white sand that will keep the clay from cracking as it dries.

After the storyteller dolls have been formed, they are allowed to air dry up to a week. Then the dolls are ready to be fired (baked in a hot oven.) Firing makes the pieces strong.

A Pueblo storyteller doll can be a woman, a man, or even an animal.

HOW-TO PROJECT

Storyteller dolls can be sculpted from any kind of clay. Self-hardening clay dries in the air. Other types of clay may have to be baked in an oven. Be sure to follow the directions on the package.

Whatever type of clay you use, you must join the pieces together with water. Dip your fingers in water, and moisten the clay on both surfaces to be joined. The water bonds the clay parts so they will not fall apart when they dry.

You need:

Self-hardening or other clay
Small bowl with water
Newspaper to work on
Poster paints or acrylics
Paintbrush

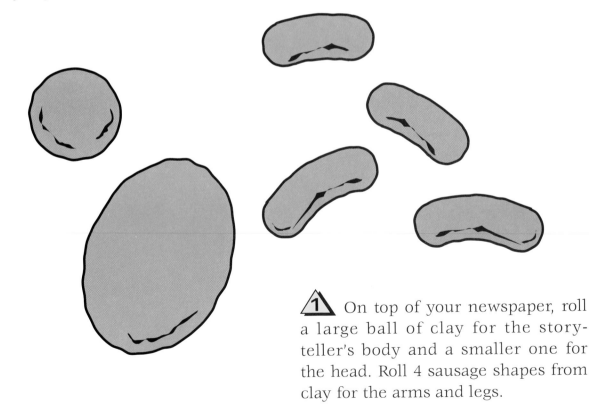

1 On top of your newspaper, roll a large ball of clay for the story-teller's body and a smaller one for the head. Roll 4 sausage shapes from clay for the arms and legs.

2 Join the pieces together with water. Bend and sculpt the pieces a little, so that the storyteller is in a sitting position with open arms.

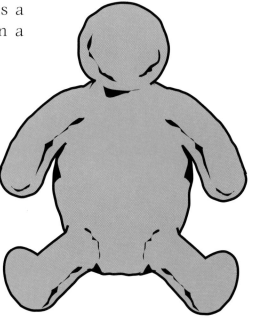

3 Roll smaller balls of clay to form a child's body and head. Roll small sausage shapes for the child's arms and legs. Join the pieces together as in steps 1 and 2. Make as many children as you like, and attach them to the storyteller's body—on her lap and in her arms.

△4 Smooth and shape the figures with water. Sculpt the dolls any way you like.

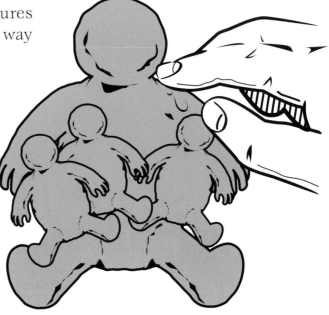

△5 When the clay is dry, paint your figures with poster paints or acrylics. A traditional storyteller doll has closed eyes and an open mouth.

WHAT ELSE YOU CAN DO

Be Creative: In step 4 you can add pieces of clay for a hat or clothing. Or scratch in lines with a toothpick, fork, or other tool.

Paper Storyteller: Cut a storyteller doll from construction paper. Cut separate smaller figures and glue them to the larger doll.

Tell Stories: Find books at your library that contain Pueblo stories. Tell the stories to your family and friends.

Chumash Basket

You can use your baskets to hold seashells, candy, jewelry—or whatever you like!

CHUMASH BASKETS

Baskets woven from plant materials have always been essential to the Chumash (CHOO-mash) Indians of California's southwestern coast. The earliest Chumash used baskets for preparing, cooking, and storing food. They also used baskets in ceremonies. They learned the best time of year to collect the plants they needed. Chumash basketmakers pick reeds and grasses when they are most bendable or twigs and roots when they are full of moisture.

The Chumash live in the California-Intermountain culture area. Their first settlements were located on the coast, including many islands off the seashore. Plants are an important part of the Chumash way of life. They harvest the roots, seeds, leaves, and flowers they need for food, medicine, and ceremonies.

TECHNIQUE

The early Chumash developed a unique method of making baskets for cooking acorns—one of their major food sources. Women coiled dried grasses and willow twigs into circular bowls, binding the coils with thin plant threads. Strands of grass—dyed black, or in naturally contrasting colors—were woven into the baskets to form patterns. After weaving the baskets, the Chumash made them watertight by swirling hot tar around the insides. They used lumps of tar that had washed up on beaches from natural tar springs in the ocean.

Chumash girls learn basketweaving from their mothers and grandmothers. The girls first learn to make plain baskets. When they become more skilled, they weave in patterns.

HOW-TO PROJECT

Make a basket with raffia, a natural material obtained from palm leaves.

About Raffia: Raffia can be found in craft stores, school supply stores and catalogs, and some flower shops. It may be worked dry or damp, although damp raffia will give your basket a smoother look. To dampen, soak raffia in water for about two hours and pat with a paper towel.

Adding On: Your raffia strands will not be long enough to complete your basket. Lengthen a bunch of raffia by covering about two inches of the old bunch with a new bunch and coiling them together. To lengthen a single strand of raffia for sewing, work a few inches with the end of the old strand together with a new strand or simply tie the strands together with a knot.

You need:

Raffia
A blunt needle with a large eye
Scissors

1 Gather 8 strands of raffia into a bunch so they are even at one end. Tie the ends together with another strand of raffia. Thread the other end of that strand into the needle.

2 Coil the bunched raffia into a tight curl. Sew two coils together by first bringing the single raffia strand over the top of the outside coil, then down through the inside coil. Keep coiling the bunched raffia and stitching it together about every ½ inch. Always pull the thread tight.

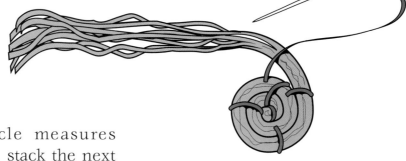

3 When the circle measures about 4 inches across, stack the next bunched row on top of the previous one, instead of placing it next to it. This will build up the sides of the basket. Continue building up more rows until the sides are at least 2 inches high.

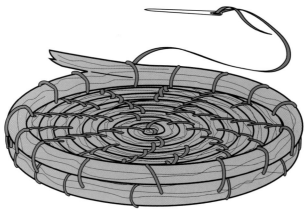

4 To finish the basket smoothly, cut the bunched raffia at an angle. Sew down the tapered ends. Then take an extra two or three stitches inside the basket and trim away the loose end of your sewing strand.

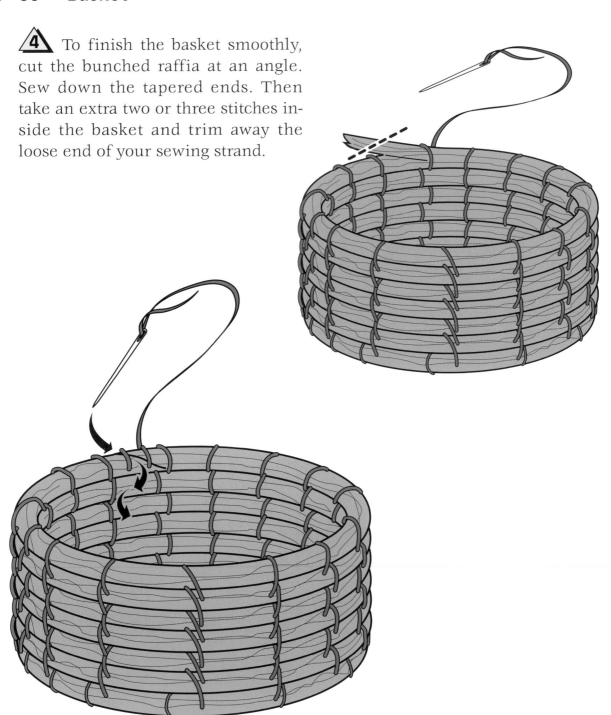

WHAT ELSE YOU CAN DO

Color and Patterns: Raffia can be bought already colored, or you can dye it by dipping it into food coloring. Colored raffia can be stitched to the outside of the basket to form diamonds, zigzags, and other geometric patterns. First outline the pattern with marker. Then thread a needle with a length of raffia and fill in the area by stitching over each coil.

Coloring patterns on your basket is even simpler than overstitching with raffia. Add designs to your finished basket with poster paints or markers.

Other Shapes: Design bigger baskets, or baskets with slanted or curved sides. For a basket with slanted sides, complete the flat bottom circle. Then press each coil up and out instead of straight up.

Haida Totem Pole

Use construction paper to make raven beaks, whale fins, and other decorations for your totem pole.

TOTEM POLES

In the northwestern continental United States, and in western Canada and Alaska, many native villages display totem poles. The poles are markers that represent a village or a single house. The carvings on the poles are images of a family's "crest." A crest is a symbol, often of an animal or mythical creature, that is associated with that family or clan.

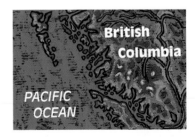

The Haida (HY-duh) live in the Northwest Coast culture area. Many kinds of tall trees grow in the area. The Haida use the trees—such as cedar, redwood, and fir—to make totem poles, boats, and masks.

TECHNIQUE

Making a totem pole begins with a careful search for a straight red cedar tree. The tree is cut down, and the bark, branches, and top are cut off.

Before carving the pole, the carver draws a design on paper. Then he creates the design by cutting away parts of the log. He might also add pieces of wood for the fins of a fish, or the beak and wings of a bird. When he is finished carving, he paints the totem pole in the tribe's traditional colors.

A totem pole may be up to 80 feet tall. A carver works on a log as it lies on its side. Then a crane is used to raise the pole upright. The whole community celebrates the raising of the totem pole with music, dancing, and feasting.

The image of a raven is often seen on Haida totem poles. The raven is an important part of the mythology of Northwest Coast tribes.

A common story among the tribes tells how long ago darkness covered the earth, because a powerful chief kept daylight in a box. Raven tricked his way into the chief's household. He stole the daylight ball and gave light to all people.

Raven is also called a trickster because he likes to play practical jokes on others. Once in a while, his tricks backfire on him.

HOW-TO PROJECT

Make a totem pole with three raven beaks from paper.

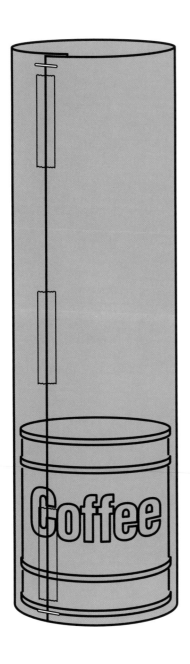

1 Roll the tag board around the coffee can and staple the ends. Tape at several points in between the staples until the tube is sturdy.

2 Cut the colored paper into 3 pieces measuring 12 by 18 inches. Cut 6 more pieces that measure 5 by 8 inches. You may cut the large and small pieces from the same color paper or from contrasting colors.

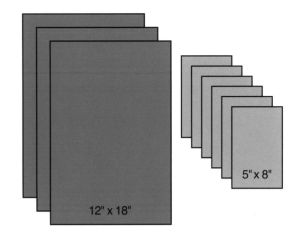

3 To make each raven beak, fold two of the 5-by-8-inch rectangles in half. Cut away one corner of each rectangle in a curve.

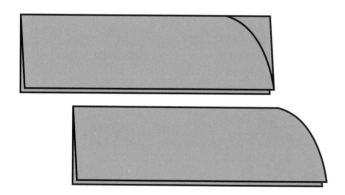

4 On the end opposite the curve, make a cut about ½ inch long on each of the folded edges. Bend the paper down, forming tabs.

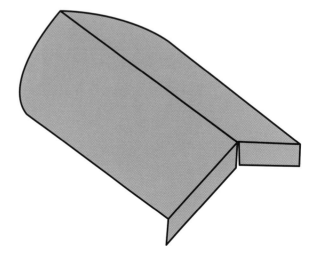

5 Tape the curved edges together on each piece. Place the tape inside, so it doesn't show. You now have one upper and one lower raven's beak.

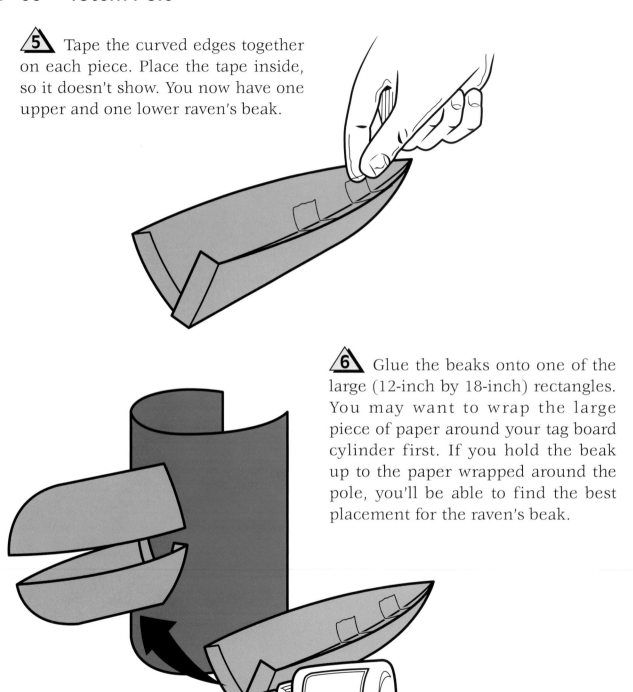

6 Glue the beaks onto one of the large (12-inch by 18-inch) rectangles. You may want to wrap the large piece of paper around your tag board cylinder first. If you hold the beak up to the paper wrapped around the pole, you'll be able to find the best placement for the raven's beak.

7 Repeat steps 3 to 6 to make two more ravens. Cut eyes and other shapes from paper and glue them to the raven faces. Or draw features and shapes patterned after Haida designs. Wrap each raven around the tag board pole and tape securely in back.

WHAT ELSE YOU CAN DO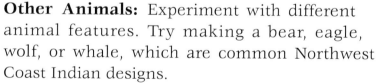

Other Animals: Experiment with different animal features. Try making a bear, eagle, wolf, or whale, which are common Northwest Coast Indian designs.

Masks: Instead of wrapping your raven face around a pole, make it into a mask. Hang huge raven masks from large pieces of paper as wall decorations. Or make a movable mask you can wear. Tie a string to both sides of the mask, so you can tie it around your head. Attach another string to the front of the lower beak. When you pull the string, the beak will open.

Weights: Put stones or other weights inside the coffee can to make your totem pole more stable.

METRIC CONVERSION CHART

If you want to use the metric system, convert measurements using the chart on the right. Because fractions can be hard to work with, round all metric measurements to the nearest whole number.

when you know:	multiply by:	to find:
Length		
inches	25.00	millimeters
inches	2.54	centimeters
feet	30.00	centimeters
feet	.30	meters
yards	.91	meters
miles	1.61	kilometers
Volume		
teaspoons	5.00	milliliters
tablespoons	15.00	milliliters
fluid ounces	30.00	milliliters
cups	0.24	liters
pints	0.47	liters
quarts	0.95	liters
gallons	3.80	liters
Weight		
ounces	28.00	grams
pounds	0.45	kilograms

GLOSSARY

adobe: A building material made of mud or clay mixed with straw

artisan: A person who is very skilled at making crafts

bison: A large animal of the North American plains, which in the past was often hunted for food and for its hide. Bison are often incorrectly called "buffalo."

clan: A group of relatives with a common ancestor

crest: A symbol that is associated with a family or clan and its history. Crests are often animals or mythical creatures.

culture: The customs, ideas, and traditions of a certain group of people. Culture includes religious celebrations, arts and crafts, folktales, costumes, and food.

culture area: A group of tribes with similar cultures, or the area where this group lives

fiesta: A festival celebrated in Mexican and some Southwest cultures

geometric patterns: Patterns that use simple shapes, such as circles, triangles, or squares

nation: Another word for tribe. "Nation" can also refer to a group of tribes who have united through an agreement of cooperation.

pueblo: The Spanish word for "village." Native American settlements of the Southwest are called pueblos.

raffia: The dried fiber of the raffia palm tree leaf

reservation: An area of land that Indian people have kept through agreement with the U.S. government

sinew: Cord made from tendons, the tissue in an animal's body that connects muscles to bones

symmetrical: Appearing the same on opposite sides

totem pole: A cedar log carved with clan or family crests. Totem poles are made in native cultures of the Pacific Northwest and Alaska.

tribe: A large group of people who traditionally lived in the same area, spoke the same language, and were led by a chief and a council of elders

READ MORE ABOUT NATIVE NORTH AMERICA

Fiction & Folktales

Bierhorst, John, ed. *On the Road of Stars: Native American Night Poems and Sleep Charms,* illustrations by Judy Pedersen. New York: Macmillan, 1994.

DePaola, Tomie. *The Legend of the Indian Paintbrush,* illustrations by the author. New York: G. P. Putnam's Sons, 1988.

Goble, Paul. *Iktomi and the Buzzard,* illustrations by the author. New York: Orchard, 1994.

Mayo, Gretchen. *Meet Tricky Coyote!* illustrations by the author. New York: Walker, 1993.

McDermott, Gerald. *Arrow to the Sun: A Pueblo Indian Tale,* illustrations by the author. New York: Viking, 1974.

McDermott, Gerald. *Raven: A Trickster Tale from the Pacific Northwest,* illustrations by the author. San Diego: Harcourt Brace Jovanovich, 1993.

Oliviero, Jamie. *The Day the Sun Was Stolen,* illustrations by Sharon Hitchcock. New York: Hyperion Books for Children, 1995.

Sneve, Virginia Driving Hawk, ed. *Dancing Teepees: Poems of American Indian Youth,* illustrations by Stephen Gammell. New York: Holiday House, 1989.

Weisman, Joan. *The Storyteller,* illustrations by David P. Bradley. New York: Rizzoli, 1993.

Nonfiction

Hoyt-Goldsmith, Diane. *Pueblo Storyteller,* photographs by Lawrence Migdale. New York: Holiday House, 1991.

Hunter, Sally. *Four Seasons of Corn: A Winnebago Tradition,* photographs by Joe Allen. Minneapolis: Lerner Publications, 1997.

Jensen, Vickie. *Carving a Totem Pole,* photographs by the author. New York: Henry Holt, 1996.

Keegan, Marcia. *Pueblo Boy: Growing Up in Two Worlds,* photographs by the author. New York: Cobblehill Books, 1991.

King, Sandra. *Shannon: An Ojibway Dancer,* photographs by Catherine Whipple. Minneapolis: Lerner Publications, 1993.

Littlechild, George. *This Land Is My Land,* illustrations by the author. New York: HarperCollins, 1993.

Moore, Reavis. *Native Artists of North America.* Santa Fe: John Muir, 1993.

Roessel, Monty. *Songs from the Loom: A Navajo Girl Learns to Weave,* photographs by the author. Minneapolis: Lerner Publications, 1995.

Swentzell, Rina. *Children of Clay: A Family of Pueblo Potters,* photographs by Bill Steen. Minneapolis: Lerner Publications, 1993.

Yamane, Linda. *Weaving a California Tradition: A Native American Basketmaker,* photographs by Dugan Aguilar. Minneapolis: Lerner Publications, 1996.

INDEX

ABOUT THE AUTHOR

Florence Temko is an internationally known author of more than 30 books on world folkcrafts and paper arts. She has traveled in 31 countries, gaining much of her skill firsthand. Ms. Temko shows her enthusiasm for crafts through simple, inventive adaptations of traditional arts and crafts projects. She has presented hundreds of hands-on programs in schools and museums, including the Metropolitan Museum of Art in New York City, and at many education conferences across the country. She lives in San Diego, California.

ACKNOWLEDGMENTS

The photographs in this book are reproduced with the permission of:

p. 6 (left), Turkish Republic, Ministry of Culture and Tourism; p. 6 (right), Wilford Archaeology Laboratory, University of Minnesota, by Kathy Raskob/IPS; p. 7 (left), Nelson-Atkins Museum, Kansas City, Missouri; p. 7 (right), Freer Gallery of Art, Smithsonian Institution; pp. 8, 9, 12, 18, 24, 30, 34, 40, 46, 52, Robert L. and Diane Wolfe; p. 13, © Catherine Whipple; pp. 19, 25, 41 (both), Images International/Bud Nielsen; p. 29 (both), © Steven Ferry; p. 35, © David Burckhalter; p. 47, Dugan Aguilar, Courtesy of California State Indian Museum; p. 53, © Monica Brown.

The maps and illustrations on pages 2, 11, 12, 13, 18, 24, 30, 34, 40, 46, 52, and 53 are by John Erste.

The illustration on page 2 is based on a Blackfeet beadwork design.